Contents

Key
* easy
** medium
*** difficult

Mexican food

Mexico is the most southerly country in North America. Its capital, Mexico City, is one of the largest cities in the world.

Mexican people love cooking and eating. Mexican food is tasty, and it has lots of dishes that are easy to make.

In the past

Historians believe that people have been farming in Mexico for over 5000 years. Early Mexicans, among them the Mayans and Aztecs, grew a wide range of crops, many of which were unknown in Europe. Their cooking ingredients included turkey, sweetcorn, tomatoes, peppers, chillies, squashes (such as pumpkin and courgette), peanuts, avocados, guavas, chocolate and vanilla.

Mexico

Julie McCulloch

Heinemann

www.heinemann.co.uk
Visit our website to find out more information about **Heinemann Library** books.

To order:
☎ Phone 44 (0) 1865 888066
▤ Send a fax to 44 (0) 1865 314091
▭ Visit the Heinemann Bookshop at www.heinemann.co.uk to browse our catalogue and order online.

First published in Great Britain by Heinemann Library, Halley Court, Jordan Hill, Oxford OX2 8EJ, a division of Reed Educational and Professional Publishing Ltd. Heinemann is a registered trademark of Reed Educational & Professional Publishing Limited.

OXFORD MELBOURNE AUCKLAND JOHANNESBURG BLANTYRE
GABORONE IBADAN PORTSMOUTH NH (USA) CHICAGO

Designed by Tinstar Design (www.tinstar.co.uk)
Illustrations by Nicholas Beresford-Davies
Originated by Dot Gradations
Printed by Wing King Tong in Hong Kong

ISBN 0 431 11702 0   (hardback)   ISBN 0 431 11709 8   (paperback)
06 05 04 03 02   06 05 04 03 02
10 9 8 7 6 5 4 3 2   10 9 8 7 6 5 4 3 2 1

British Library Cataloguing in Publication Data
McCulloch, Julie
    Mexico. – (A world of recipes)
    1. Cookery, Mexican – Juvenile literature 2.Mexico –
    Description and travel – Juvenile literature
    I. Title
    641.5'123'0972

Acknowledgements
The Publishers would like to thank the following for permission to reproduce photographs:
Corbis, p.5. All other photographs: Gareth Boden.
Illustration p.45, US Department of Agriculture/US Department of Health and Human Services.

Cover photographs reproduced with permission of Gareth Boden.

Our thanks to Sue Townsend, home economist, and Sue Mildenhall for their comments in the preparation of this book.

Every effort has been made to contact copyright holders of any material reproduced in this book. Any omissions will be rectified in subsequent printings if notice is given to the Publisher.

Words appearing in the text in bold, **like this**, are explained in the glossary.

In 1519, Mexico was conquered by Spain. The Spanish brought many new ingredients, such as milk, cheese, chicken, rice, wheat, cinnamon, oranges and peaches. Today, Mexican cooking is a mixture of these different influences.

Around the country

The geography of Mexico is ideal for producing a huge range of food. The landscape varies from dry deserts in the north, through high mountains in the centre of the country, to **tropical** jungles in the south-east.

▲ *These chillies growing in a Mexican field will be used in many different dishes.*

Different kinds of food are produced in different areas. In the north cattle are raised for beef. Many different kinds of fruit and vegetables are grown in the cool mountainous areas in the middle of the country. The hotter areas in the south and around the coast produce tropical fruit such as papayas, pineapples and coconuts. The sea provides fish and shellfish.

Mexican meals

Most people in Mexico eat their main meal at lunchtime. This meal, called comida, traditionally consists of three courses – a starter, a main course and a pudding. Comida is often followed by a siesta – a short nap.

For breakfast, many Mexicans have coffee with milk, some sweet rolls and maybe some yoghurt. The early evening meal (merienda) is usually a light snack, such as cereal, sweet bread or tortillas and hot chocolate. The day ends with cena, a light supper, which can be left-overs from comida, a potato and onion omelette, or a sandwich.

Ingredients

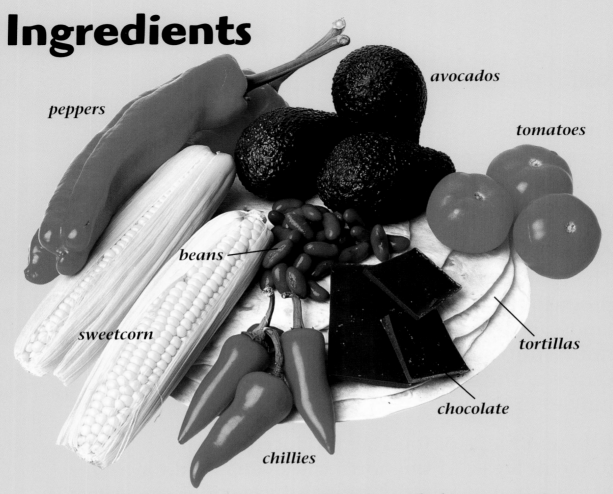

peppers

avocados

tomatoes

beans

sweetcorn

tortillas

chocolate

chillies

The ingredients for most Mexican dishes are quite easy to find in supermarkets and shops. Here are some of the most common ones.

Avocados

Avocados originally came from Central and South America. The name avocado comes from the Mexican word 'ahuacatl'. Avocados are a fruit, not a vegetable, and have a very large stone in the centre.

Beans

Different beans are used in many Mexican recipes. Two of the most common types of beans are butter beans (used in the recipe on page 22) and kidney beans (used in the recipe on page 26). They are easiest to use if you buy them in cans.

⚠ Chillies

Chillies are spicy peppers used in many Mexican dishes. There are hundreds of different sorts – some are quite mild, and others are very, very hot! Fresh chillies contain an oil that can make your eyes and skin sting if it touches them, so it is a good idea to use chilli powder, made from ground-up dried chillies, rather than fresh ones. If you don't like spicy food, just leave out the chilli powder.

Chocolate

Chocolate has been eaten and drunk in Mexico for thousands of years. It is made from the roasted, crushed beans of the cocoa plant. In Mexico, chocolate is made into hot drinks, used in puddings, and used in savoury sauces. Plain, dark chocolate is the best sort to use in Mexican recipes.

Sweetcorn

Sweetcorn was one of the first plants grown in Mexico, and it is used in many dishes. You can buy fresh sweetcorn 'on the cob' (still in the leafy case in which it grows), frozen 'on the cob', or separated from the cob (frozen or canned).

Tomatoes

Tomatoes are used in many Mexican recipes. You can use either fresh or canned tomatoes in the recipes in this book.

Tortillas

Tortillas are flat circles of bread. They are eaten with many different meals in Mexico. Two different types of tortillas are eaten in Mexico – wheat tortillas (which contain wheat flour) and corn tortillas (which contain flour made from ground sweetcorn). Sweetcorn flour can be difficult to find, so the recipe for tortillas in this book is for wheat tortillas.

Before you start

Kitchen rules

There are a few basic rules you should always follow when you are cooking.

- Ask an adult if you can use the kitchen.

- Some cooking processes, especially those involving hot water or oil, can be dangerous. When you see this sign, take extra care or ask an adult to help.
- Wash your hands before you start.
- Wear an apron to protect your clothes, and tie back long hair.
- Be very careful when using sharp knives.
- Never leave pan handles sticking out in case you knock them.
- Always wear oven gloves to lift things in and out of the oven.
- Wash fruit and vegetables before you use them.

How long will it take?

Some of the recipes in this book are quick and easy, and some are more difficult and take longer. The strip across the top of the right hand page of each recipe tells you how long it will take you to cook each dish from start to finish. It also shows how difficult each dish is to make: every recipe is either * (easy), ** (medium) or *** (difficult).

Quantities and measurements

You can see how many people each recipe will serve at the top of the right hand page, too. Most of the recipes in this book make enough to feed two people. Where it is more sensible to make a larger amount, though, the recipe makes enough for four. You can multiply or divide the quantities if you want to cook for more or fewer people.

Ingredients for recipes can be measured in two different ways. Metric measurements use grams and millilitres. Imperial measurements use ounces and fluid ounces. This book uses metric measurements. If you want to convert these into imperial measurements, see the chart on page 44.

In the recipes you will see the following abbreviations:

tbsp = tablespoon
tsp = teaspoon

g = grams
ml = millilitres

Utensils

To cook the recipes in this book, you will need these utensils (as well as kitchen essentials such as spoons, plates and bowls):

- baking tray
- chopping board
- foil
- food processor or blender
- frying pan
- grater
- large, flat, ovenproof dish
- measuring jug

- potato masher
- rolling pin
- saucepan with lid
- set of scales
- sharp knife
- sieve or colander
- wooden cocktail sticks

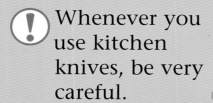

⚠ Whenever you use kitchen knives, be very careful.

Tortillas

Tortillas are eaten with many Mexican meals. Sometimes they are served as an accompaniment to the meal, but often they form part of the meal itself, usually by being wrapped around different fillings.

What you need

100g plain flour
  (+ a few extra
  tbsp to sprinkle
  on the chopping
  board)
½ tsp salt
2 tbsp olive oil

The recipes for cheese-filled enchiladas (page 20) and fish burritos (page 30) use tortillas, so you will need to make some tortillas before cooking these dishes. You can also buy ready-made tortillas, but here is how to make your own.

What you do

1 Put the flour and salt into a mixing bowl. Mix in the oil with a spoon, then gradually stir in 4 tbsp warm water until the mixture starts to form a dough.

2 Sprinkle some flour onto a chopping board. **Knead** the dough on the board until it is smooth.

3 Divide the dough into four pieces, to make four tortillas.

4 Shape one piece of dough into a ball, then flatten it.

5 Sprinkle some more flour onto the board and onto a rolling pin. Roll out the ball of dough into a circle, until the dough is as thin as you can make it without breaking it.

6 Heat a frying pan until it sizzles when you sprinkle a drop of water into it. Put the tortilla into the pan.

7 Cook the tortilla for one minute, then turn it over and cook the other side for 30 seconds. Slide the cooked tortilla out of the pan onto a plate.

8 Repeat steps 4 to 7 with the other three pieces of dough.

STORING TORTILLAS

You can store your tortillas to use later. Put a square of greaseproof paper between each tortilla so that they don't stick together. Leave them to **cool**, then put the stack of tortillas into a plastic bag. They will keep for several days in the fridge.

Guacamole

Guacamole is eaten all over Mexico. It can be eaten as a snack, spread on tortillas, or used as an accompaniment to other dishes.

What you need

1 onion
handful fresh
    coriander leaves
    (see box below)
¼ tsp chilli powder
    (optional)
1 avocado
1 tbsp lemon juice

What you do

1 **Peel** the skin from the onion, and finely **chop** half of it.

2 Finely chop the fresh coriander.

3 In a bowl, mix together the chopped onion, coriander and chilli powder (if you are using it).

4 Cut the avocado in half lengthways. Use a spoon to remove the stone.

5 Use the spoon to scoop out the flesh of the avocado into the bowl, leaving the skin behind.

6 Add the lemon juice to the mixture.

7 **Mash** all the ingredients together with a fork.

CORIANDER

Coriander is a herb that looks a bit like parsley. It is used a lot in Mexican cooking. You will usually find fresh coriander in the fruit and vegetable section of supermarkets. If you can't find any, try using fresh parsley leaves instead. Don't substitute dried coriander, though. This is made from the seeds, rather than the leaves, of the coriander plant, and tastes completely different!

Nachos

Nachos are fried tortillas baked with guacamole (page 12), cheese and soured cream. It is almost impossible to eat nachos with a knife and fork! The best way to eat them is with your fingers.

Frying tortillas can be dangerous, as it involves dropping tortillas into a pan of very hot oil. This recipe suggests using ready-made fried tortillas which are sold in bags, like crisps. They are called tostadas in Mexico, but are often called 'tortilla chips' elsewhere.

What you need

1 portion guacamole
1 small bag tortilla chips
50g hard cheese (for example Cheddar)
50ml soured cream

What you do

1 Make the guacamole, following the recipe on page 12.

2 **Grate** the cheese into a small bowl.

3 Put the tortilla chips into a large, flat, ovenproof dish.

4 Spoon the guacamole over the tortilla chips.

5 Spoon the soured cream over the guacamole.

6 Finally, sprinkle the grated cheese over the soured cream.

(!) 7 Put the dish under the **grill** for about 5 minutes, or until the soured cream is bubbling and the cheese has melted.

NACHOS WITH BEANS

A delicious variation to this recipe for nachos is to add kidney beans. Put 2 tbsp of canned kidney beans into a bowl, and roughly **mash** them with a fork. Spread the mashed beans over the tortilla chips before adding the guacamole, soured cream and cheese.

Corn soup

Hot soup is often served in the cold, mountainous regions of Mexico. Most lunches start with a bowl of soup, and many evening meals consist of soup served with a stack of tortillas. This simple corn soup is full of flavour and very **nourishing**.

If you use the frozen sweetcorn, you need to **thaw** it before you use it. You can do this in two ways:

a) Take it out of the freezer at least an hour before you want to use it, and leave it to stand;

b) Pour hot water over the sweetcorn, leave it to stand for a couple of minutes, then carefully empty the sweetcorn into a colander or sieve to **drain**.

What you need

1 tbsp sunflower oil
1 onion
1 red pepper
225g canned or
    frozen sweetcorn
    (thawed)
1 vegetable stock cube
125ml single cream

What you do

1 **Peel** the skin from the onion, and finely **chop** half of it.

2 Cut the red pepper in half, then scoop out the seeds. Chop half of the flesh into strips.

3 Put 400ml water into a saucepan, and bring it to the **boil**. Crumble the stock cube into the water, and stir until it **dissolves**. Put the stock to one side.

4 Heat the oil in a saucepan. **Fry** the chopped onion and red pepper for about 5 minutes.

5 Put the onion and pepper mixture and the sweetcorn into a blender or food processor. **Blend** until smooth.

6 Put the mixture back into the saucepan, and add the stock.

7 **Simmer** the soup for about 5 minutes, until it is hot.

8 Stir in the cream. You can use the other half of the red pepper to garnish your soup.

COLD SOUP

This dish can also be served cold for a refreshing summer soup. Let the soup **cool**, then put it into the fridge for a couple of hours before serving it.

Grilled corn on the cob with salsa

Corn cobs can be eaten on their own or with a sauce. This recipe shows you how to make corn cobs with salsa, which is a spicy Mexican sauce made with tomatoes and fruit. Mexican people eat salsa with many different dishes. In Mexican restaurants, you often find a bowl of salsa on the table along with the salt and pepper.

What you need

2 corn cobs
2 tbsp sunflower oil
1 onion
¼ tsp chilli powder
  (if you are using it)
1 slice canned
  pineapple
2 tomatoes
1 red pepper

What you do

1 **Peel** the skin from the onion and finely **chop** half of it.

2 Chop the tomatoes into small pieces.

3 Scoop the seeds from the red pepper, and chop half the flesh into strips.

4 Chop the slice of pineapple into small pieces.

5 Heat 1 tbsp of the oil in a saucepan over a medium heat. Add the chopped onion and the chilli powder (if you are using any). **Fry** for 5 minutes until the onion is soft.

6 Add the chopped tomatoes, red pepper and pineapple. Turn the heat down to low, and **cover** the pan. Leave the salsa to **simmer** for about 10 minutes, stirring occasionally.

7 While the salsa is cooking, brush the remaining 1 tbsp of oil onto the corn cobs.

8 Put them on a baking tray under a hot **grill** for about 10 minutes, turning them occasionally so they are cooked on all sides.

9 Put the corn cobs onto plates, and spoon half of the salsa sauce onto each plate.

HOT AND SALTY

For a really quick snack, try making corn cobs with butter and salt. Grill the corn cobs as described above, then spread butter on them while they are still hot, so it melts into the corn. Sprinkle them with salt, and eat them straight away. Take care they don't burn the inside of your mouth, though!

Cheese-filled enchiladas

What you need

4 tortillas (bought or
   home-made)

For the filling:
100g hard cheese (for
   example Cheddar)
250g cottage cheese

For the tomato sauce:
1 tbsp sunflower oil
½ onion
1 clove garlic
150g tomatoes

Enchiladas are tortillas rolled around a filling. These cheesy enchiladas are served with a hot tomato sauce.

What you do

1 Make 4 tortillas (see page 10). You can also buy them ready-made.

2 **Preheat** the oven to 190°C/375°F/gas mark 5.

3 **Peel** the skin from the onion and the garlic clove, and finely **chop** them.

4 Chop the tomatoes into small pieces.

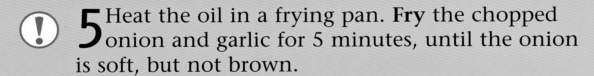

5 Heat the oil in a frying pan. **Fry** the chopped onion and garlic for 5 minutes, until the onion is soft, but not brown.

6 Add the chopped tomatoes. **Cover** the pan, and **simmer** the mixture for about 20 minutes, stirring occasionally.

DIFFERENT FILLINGS

You can make enchiladas with all sorts of different fillings. Here are some ideas:
- guacamole (see page 12)
- picadillo (see page 24)
- chilli con carne (see page 26)

7 While the tomato sauce is simmering, **grate** the hard cheese. Mix ⅔ of the hard cheese with all of the cottage cheese in a bowl. (Keep the rest of the hard cheese for later.)

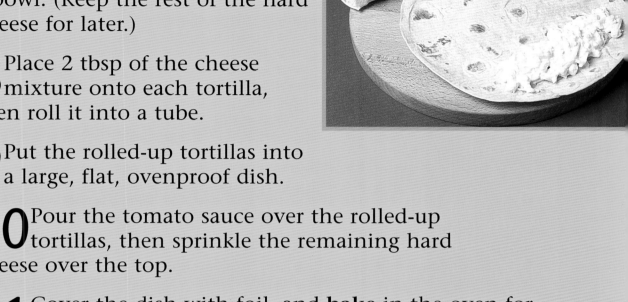

8 Place 2 tbsp of the cheese mixture onto each tortilla, then roll it into a tube.

9 Put the rolled-up tortillas into a large, flat, ovenproof dish.

10 Pour the tomato sauce over the rolled-up tortillas, then sprinkle the remaining hard cheese over the top.

11 Cover the dish with foil, and **bake** in the oven for 30 minutes. Remove the foil and bake for a further 15 minutes until the cheese is brown and bubbling.

Bean and potato patties

Beans are eaten in many different ways in Mexico. These bean and potato patties are good served with spicy salsa (see recipe on page 18).

What you need

250g potatoes
60g hard cheese (for example Cheddar)
1 egg
125g canned butter beans
2 tbsp flour
½ tbsp sunflower oil

What you do

1 Carefully **peel** the potatoes using a sharp knife, then cut them into small pieces.

2 Put the potatoes into a saucepan full of water, and **boil** them for about 15 minutes until they are soft.

3 While the potatoes are boiling, **grate** the cheese into a small bowl.

4 Crack the egg into a bowl. **Beat** it with a fork or a whisk until the yolk and the white are mixed.

5 When the potatoes are soft, **drain** them by emptying the pan into a colander or sieve. Put the drained potatoes back into the pan.

6 Drain the butter beans and put them into the pan with the potatoes. **Mash** the potatoes and beans together with a fork or a potato masher.

7 Add the grated cheese and beaten egg to the mashed potatoes and beans. Mix everything together well.

8 Divide the mixture into four pieces, and shape each piece into a flattened round patty.

9 Sprinkle the flour onto a chopping board. Turn the patties over a couple of times on the board to coat them in flour.

(!) **10** Heat the oil in a frying pan over a low heat. Put the patties into the pan, and **fry** them gently for 10 minutes. Turn them over carefully, and fry on the other side for another 10 minutes.

Picadillo

What you need

½ onion
1 garlic clove
1 apple
1 tbsp sunflower oil
150g tomatoes
200g minced beef
¼ tsp chilli powder
   (optional)
25g raisins
½ tsp cinnamon
½ tsp cumin

Picadillo is a main course dish made from minced beef, fruit and spices. It is usually served with long grain rice or tortillas.

What you do

1 Peel the skin from the onion and the garlic clove, and **chop** finely.

2 Using a sharp knife, carefully cut the apple into pieces. Don't use the core of the apple.

3 Chop the tomatoes into small pieces.

(!) 4 Heat the oil in a frying pan over a medium heat. Add the minced beef, and the chopped onion and garlic.

5 Fry the mixture for 15 minutes, stirring occasionally, until the onion is soft and the beef is brown.

6 Add the chopped apple, chopped tomatoes, chilli powder (if using any), raisins, cinnamon and cumin to the pan.

7 **Cover** the pan and cook the picadillo over a low heat for about 15 minutes, stirring occasionally.

PICADILLO-STUFFED PEPPERS

Picadillo is sometimes served stuffed into red peppers. This looks impressive, but is easy to do! Carefully cut the top off a red pepper, and scoop out the seeds. Spoon the cooked picadillo into the hollow pepper, replace the pepper's top and **bake** in a medium oven for about 40 minutes.

25

Chilli con carne

'Chilli con carne' means 'chillies with meat'. Chillies are an important part of many Mexican dishes. In the past, Mexican people believed that chillies could cure many illnesses, including toothache and ear-ache. Modern science has proved that chillies do contain lots of healthy **vitamins**. Serve chilli con carne with long grain rice.

What you need

1 tbsp sunflower oil
200g lean minced beef
1 onion
1 clove garlic
½ tsp chilli powder
   (optional)
150g tomatoes
80g canned
   kidney beans

What you do

1 **Preheat** the oven to 160°C/325°F/gas mark 3.

2 **Peel** the skin from the onion and the garlic clove, and finely **chop** them.

3 Chop the tomatoes into small pieces.

4 Heat the oil in a frying pan over a medium heat. Add the chopped onion and garlic and the minced beef.

5 **Fry** the mixture for about 15 minutes, stirring occasionally to stop it from sticking.

6 Add the chilli powder (if you are using any), chopped tomatoes and **drained** kidney beans to the pan.

7 Cook the mixture for another 5 minutes, then pour it carefully into an ovenproof dish.

8 **Cover** the dish, and cook your chilli con carne in the oven for 1 hour.

9 Put the cooked chilli in a serving bowl. You can also serve chilli with tortillas.

VEGETARIAN VERSION – 'CHILLI SIN CARNE'

You can make a **vegetarian** version of this dish, called 'chilli sin carne' – chillies without meat! Just replace the minced beef with chopped vegetables, such as courgettes, mushrooms and red peppers.

Meat balls

The Aztec people, who lived in Mexico thousands of years ago, used to eat all sorts of animals, including dogs, frogs, snakes and armadillos! These meat balls are made from minced beef and make a tasty, filling main course.

What you need

1 slice bread
½ onion
200g minced beef
1 egg
½ tsp dried oregano
½ tsp cumin
1 tbsp sunflower oil
1 vegetable stock cube

What you do

1 To make breadcrumbs, put pieces of bread into the food processor or blender. Replace the lid and turn it onto its highest setting for a couple of minutes.

2 **Peel** the skin from the onion, and finely **chop** it.

3 Crack the egg into a bowl. **Beat** it with a fork or a whisk until the yolk and the white are mixed.

4 Put the minced beef into a large mixing bowl. Add the breadcrumbs, chopped onion, beaten egg, oregano and cumin.

5 Mix everything together with a spoon until it forms a smooth mixture.

6 Shape the mixture into balls about 4cm wide.

(!) 7 Heat the oil in a frying pan over a medium heat. **Fry** the meat balls for about 5 minutes, turning occasionally, until brown.

8 While the meat balls are frying, put 300ml water into a saucepan, and bring it to the **boil**. Crumble the stock cube into the water, and stir until it **dissolves**.

9 Pour the stock over the meat balls. Bring it to the boil, then **simmer** for 30 minutes.

10 Spoon the meat balls out onto plates, and pour a little of the stock from the pan over them.

Fish burritos

These are little parcels of fish, wrapped in tortillas. They are delicious served with guacamole (see recipe on page 12). You can use fresh or frozen cod for this recipe, but make sure frozen fish is well **thawed**.

What you need

4 tortillas
60g hard cheese (for example Cheddar)

For the filling:
1 onion
2 cod fillets (thawed if frozen)
½ tbsp sunflower oil
¼ tsp chilli powder (optional)
50ml soured cream

What you do

1 You need 4 tortillas. See page 10 to make them, or you can buy them.

2 **Preheat** the oven to 180°C/350°F/gas mark 4.

3 **Peel** the skin from the onion, and finely **chop** half of it.

4 Put the fish into a saucepan. Just cover it with water, bring to the **boil** and then **simmer** for 5 minutes.

5 **Drain** the water from the fish. Use a fork to **flake** it into a bowl, making sure you take out the skin and any bones.

6 Heat the oil in a frying pan over a medium heat. **Fry** the chopped onion and chilli powder (if you are using any) for 5 minutes, until the onion is soft. Add this mixture to the fish.

7 Add the soured cream to the fish and onions, and mix well.

8 Put a couple of spoonfuls of the fish mixture on to each tortilla, then fold the tortilla to make a square parcel (see photo on the left). Stick a cocktail stick through each parcel to keep it closed.

9 Put the parcels into an ovenproof dish.

10 **Grate** the cheese over the parcels. **Cover** the dish with foil and **bake** for 30 minutes.

11 Remove the cocktail sticks before serving.

Mexican rice

This rice dish is **nourishing** enough to serve as a main course on its own. There are two different types of rice – long and short grain. This dish works best made with long grain rice.

What you need

½ onion
1 garlic clove
150g tomatoes
1 vegetable stock cube
1 tbsp sunflower oil
125g rice
½ tsp chilli powder (optional)
60g frozen peas

What you do

1 **Peel** the skin from the onion and the garlic clove, and finely **chop** them.

2 Chop the tomatoes into small pieces.

3 Put 300ml water into a saucepan, and bring it to the **boil**. Crumble the stock cube into the water, and stir until it **dissolves**. Put the stock to one side.

4 Heat the oil in a saucepan over a medium heat. Add the chopped onions and garlic and the rice, and cook for 5 minutes, stirring all the time to stop the rice from sticking.

5 Add the chopped tomatoes, stock, chilli powder (if you are using any) and frozen peas to the pan. Bring to the boil, then reduce the heat to low.

6 **Cover** the pan and **simmer** for about 20 minutes, stirring occasionally, until all the liquid has been soaked up.

HEALTHY EXTRAS

In some regions of Mexico, rice and beans are eaten at nearly every meal. Rice and beans are both cheap ingredients, which provide a great deal of **nourishment** – **protein** from the beans, and **carbohydrate** from the rice.

Savoury fruit salad

You can serve this salad with many of the dishes in this book. It goes well with meat dishes like picadillo and chilli con carne.

What you need

1 small lettuce
1 carrot
1 apple
2 slices canned
   pineapple
1 banana
1 orange
2 tbsp lemon juice
2 tbsp sunflower oil

What you do

1 **Shred** the lettuce leaves, and put them into a salad bowl.

2 Using a sharp knife, carefully **peel** the skin from the carrot. **Grate** it into the salad bowl.

3 Cut the apple into small pieces. Don't use the core of the apple. Add the apple pieces to the salad bowl.

4 **Chop** the pineapple slices into small pieces, and add them to the salad bowl.

5 Peel the banana, then chop it into slices and add these to the bowl.

6 Peel the orange, and divide it into segments. Add these to the salad.

7 In a small bowl, mix the lemon juice and the oil. Pour this mixture over the salad as a dressing.

8 Mix, or **toss**, the salad well just before you serve it.

Rice pudding

Rice pudding is made in many different countries. This fruity Mexican version is very easy to make. There are two different sorts of rice – long and short grain. This dish works best with short grain rice, which is often called 'pudding rice' in shops.

What you need

50g rice
225ml milk
100g granulated
   sugar
40g raisins
½ tsp cinnamon
10g butter

What you do

1 Put the rice into a saucepan. Add 125ml water. Bring the water to the **boil**, then turn the heat down to low.

2 **Cover** the pan and **simmer** for about 20 minutes, until the rice has soaked up all the water and is soft.

3 Add the milk, sugar, raisins and cinnamon to the pan, and stir everything together.

4 Cook the rice pudding over a low heat, stirring all the time, until all the milk has been soaked up. This should take about 5 minutes.

5 Stir the butter into the hot rice pudding until it melts, then serve.

ADDED EXTRAS

This rice pudding tastes really good served with fruit. You could try arranging a few segments of orange or some slices of apple alongside the rice pudding when you serve it.

Cinnamon oranges

Many Mexican farmers grow oranges. This refreshing pudding is very easy to make.

What you need

2 oranges
25g caster sugar
¼ tsp ground cinnamon

What you do

1 **Peel** the skin from the oranges, then cut them into thin **slices**.

2 Place the oranges in a serving bowl.

3 Mix the sugar and the cinnamon together in a small bowl, then sprinkle them over the oranges.

4 Put the oranges, sugar and cinnamon in the fridge for at least 1 hour before serving, to **chill** them.

MEXICAN DESSERTS

Puddings and other sweet things are very popular in Mexico. Some of the most popular desserts are made from fresh fruit, often served with spices and sugar or honey, as in this dish.

MEXICAN MARKETS

Many Mexican people buy their fruit and vegetables from street markets. Most Mexican towns have a market day, or 'dia del mercado'. Markets are a good place not only to shop, but also to meet people.

Caramel custard

A version of caramel custard is made in many countries around the world. In Mexico, this dish is called 'flan'. It was probably brought to Mexico by the Spanish conquerors in the 16th century, and is now a firm favourite. This dish needs time to **chill** in the fridge, so make it several hours before you want to eat it.

What you need

60g caster sugar
225ml milk
few drops of
   vanilla essence
2 eggs, beaten

What you do

1 **Preheat** the oven to 150°C/300°F/gas mark 2.

2 Crack the eggs into a bowl. **Beat** them with a fork or a whisk until the yolk and the white are mixed.

3 Put half the sugar into a saucepan, and add 1 tbsp water. Put the saucepan over a low heat and stir gently until all the sugar has **dissolved**.

4 Turn up the heat and **boil** quickly, without stirring, until the mixture turns golden. Pour this syrup into one or two small ramekins or ovenproof dishes.

5 Heat the milk in a saucepan over a medium heat. Add the rest of the sugar and the vanilla essence. Heat for another 3 minutes, until the sugar has dissolved.

6 Stir the beaten eggs into the milk, then pour the mixture on top of the syrup.

7 Put the ramekins into a large ovenproof dish. Carefully pour hot water around them until the water reaches about halfway up their sides.

8 **Cover** the ovenproof dish with foil, then put in the oven and **bake** for 45 minutes.

(!) 9 Take the ovenproof dish out of the oven. Lift the hot ramekins of custard out of the ovenproof dish.

10 Leave the custard to **cool**, then put it into the fridge for at least 3 hours.

11 Dip the bottom of the ramekins into hot water to loosen the custard. Run a knife round the edge of the ramekins.

12 Quickly turn the custard out on to a plate before serving.

Mexican hot chocolate

The combination of plain chocolate, cinnamon and vanilla is typically Mexican. In fact, Mexican chocolate bars often have cinnamon and vanilla already added to them.

What you need

125g plain chocolate, broken into chunks
500ml milk
½ tsp ground cinnamon
few drops of vanilla essence

What you do

1 You will need either a heatproof bowl that fits on top of your saucepan, or you can melt the chocolate in the microwave, in a non-metallic, microwave proof bowl or a microwave dish.

2 Break the chocolate into pieces, and put into your bowl. Either cook on medium power in the microwave for 1 minute and 20 seconds and stir until melted. Then carry on from step 5.

3 Or put 400ml water into a saucepan. Heat the water over a medium heat until just bubbling at the edges but not **boiling**. Reduce the heat to low.

4 Put the bowl of chocolate on top and leave until melted, (about 5 minutes).

5 Warm the milk in a small saucepan. Slowly stir half the milk into the melted chocolate. Pour back into the saucepan with the rest of the milk.

6 Stir in the cinnamon and vanilla essence. Heat for a few more minutes.

7 Pour the hot chocolate into cups.

COLD CHOCOLATE

You can also use this recipe to make a cold chocolate drink. Leave the hot chocolate to **cool**, then **whisk** it with a fork or whisk before pouring it into cups.

BREAKFAST BREAD

Hot chocolate is often drunk for breakfast in Mexico. It is sometimes accompanied by pan de yema, a type of bread cooked in egg yolks, which is dipped into the hot chocolate.

Further information

Here are some places to find out more about Mexico and Mexican cooking.

Books

Cooking the Mexican Way
Rosa Coronado, First Avenue Editions, 1992
A Taste of Mexico
Linda Illsley, Thomson Learning, 1998
World Focus: Mexico
Rob Alcraft, Heinemann Library, 1996

Websites

mexconnect.com/mex_/recipes/foodindex.html
www.astray.com/recipes/?search=mexican
www.ebicom.net/%7Ehowle/page/mexidx.htm
www.lamejor.com/html/mexican_recipes.htm
www.yumyum.com/recipes.htm

Conversion chart

Ingredients for recipes can be measured in two different ways. Metric measurements use grams and millilitres. Imperial measurements use ounces and fluid ounces. This book uses metric measurements. The chart here shows you how to convert measurements from metric to imperial.

SOLIDS		LIQUIDS	
METRIC	IMPERIAL	METRIC	IMPERIAL
10g	¼ oz	30ml	1 fl oz
15g	½ oz	50ml	2 fl oz
25g	1 oz	75ml	2½ fl oz
50g	1¾ oz	100ml	3½ fl oz
75g	2¾ oz	125ml	4 fl oz
100g	3½ oz	150ml	5 fl oz
150g	5 oz	300ml	10 fl oz
250g	9 oz	600ml	20 fl oz

Healthy eating

This diagram shows which food you should eat to stay healthy. Most of your food should come from the bottom of the pyramid. Eat some of the foods from the middle every day. Only eat a little of the foods from the top.

Healthy eating, Mexican style

Mexican cooking uses many ingredients from the bottom of the pyramid – for example rice, as well as tortillas, which are flat breads made from wheat or maize flour. People also eat lots of different kinds of vegetables and beans, so you can see how healthy Mexican cooking is!

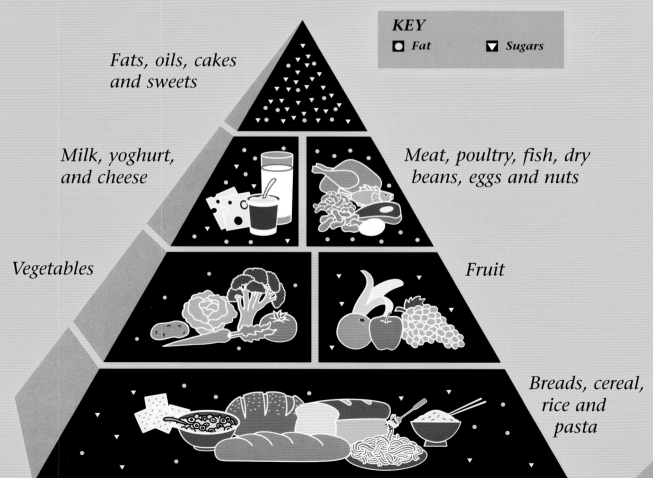

Fats, oils, cakes and sweets

KEY

☐ *Fat*   ▽ *Sugars*

Milk, yoghurt, and cheese

Meat, poultry, fish, dry beans, eggs and nuts

Vegetables

Fruit

Breads, cereal, rice and pasta

Glossary

bake cook something in the oven

beat mix something together strongly, for example egg yolks and whites

blend mix ingredients together in a blender or food processor

boil cook a liquid on the hob. Boiling liquid bubbles and steams strongly.

carbohydrate food that contains sugar and starch, such as potatoes, to give us energy

chill put a dish in the fridge for several hours before serving

chop cut something into small pieces using a knife

cool allow hot food to become cold. You should always allow food to cool before putting it in the fridge.

cover put a lid on a pan, or foil over a dish

dissolve mix something, for example sugar, until it disappears into a liquid

drain remove liquid, usually by pouring something into a colander or sieve

flake break something, for example a piece of fish, into small pieces, often using a fork

fry cook something in oil in a pan

grate break something, for example cheese, into small pieces using a grater

grill cook something under the grill

knead mix ingredients into a smooth dough, for example for bread. Kneading involves using your knuckles to make a smooth dough.

mash crush something, for example potatoes, until it is soft and pulpy

nourishing food that is good for our bodies and our health

peel remove the skin of a fruit or vegetable

preheat turn on the oven in advance, so that it is hot when you are ready to use it

protein a body building material found in some foods, such as beans, eggs and meat

shred cut or tear something, for example a lettuce, into small pieces

simmer cook a liquid on the hob. Simmering liquid bubbles and steams gently.

slice cut something into thin, flat pieces

thaw defrost something which has been frozen

toss mix ingredients, for example in a salad, quite roughly

tropical a hot, wet climate

vegetarian food that does not contain meat, or fish. People who don't eat meat or fish are called vegetarians.

vitamins our bodies get these from food to keep healthy

whisk mix ingredients using a whisk

Index